A Bug and A Prayer

A true story by Lurene Rascon

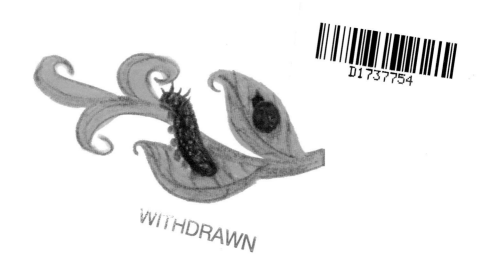

WITHDRAWN

Illustrations by McKenna Zacher

Published by The Second Page,

An imprint of Two Square Books

Long May She Wave

A BUG AND A PRAYER

Published by The Second Page, an imprint of Two Square Books Publishing

Shingle Springs, USA

FIRST EDITION

ISBN: 1505850606

Dedicated to my mother, Patricia,
for speaking powerful words to me
and showing me that God hears my prayers.

This is a simple story about an
ordinary little girl who prayed a
simple prayer— and God heard her.

It has been many years since the story
I am about to tell took place.

As with most remarkable moments in life, nothing appeared different or unusual about this day. But something was about to happen to my 6 year old self that would change my life forever.

When I wandered out on that beautiful spring day, it felt like the world was stretching its arms out wide and coming alive.

I couldn't wait to get outside, to climb the trees and dig in the dirt. I loved to lie on the grass, look at the sky and watch the clouds go by.

Our backyard was a wonderful place. It had a big, grassy patch of lawn that stretched out between the house and my dad's tool shed. Large, leafy fruit trees dotted the yard. I spent many delightful hours there.

My mom came out the back door with a basket of sheets in her arms. The clothesline stretched out above my head like giant telephone poles. As she hung the linens on the line, I remembered past summer days.

My favorite thing to do was gather the wooly, furry caterpillars. I would put them into glass jars and watch them change from caterpillars, to cocoons, to butterflies.

My dad punched holes in the tops of the jars and I filled the jars with sticks and leaves.

The caterpillars were the same kind every year. They are called Mourning Cloaks. Their bodies are black and orange with furry spikes all down their backs. The feel of their prickly feet sticking to my hands made me giggle.

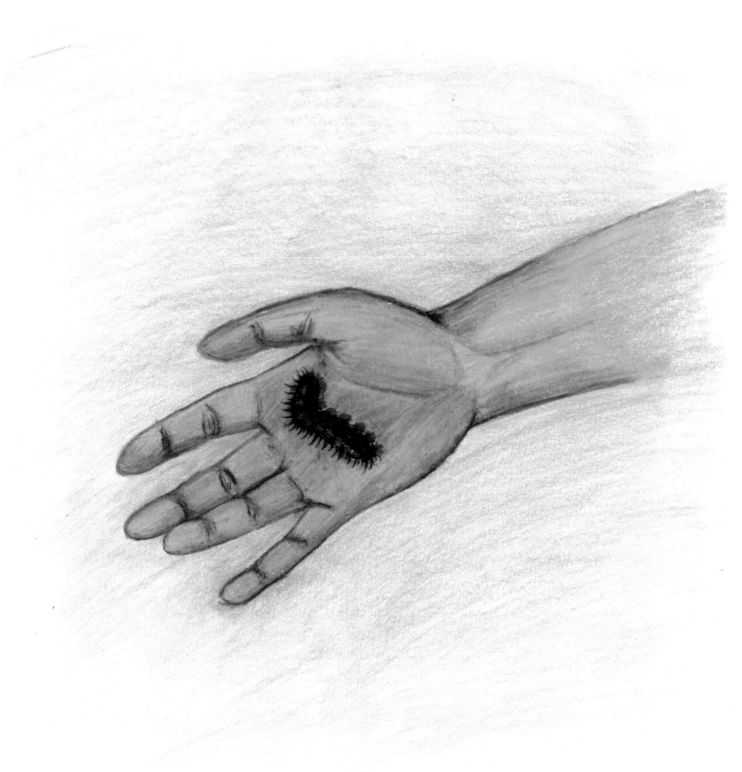

After I collected all the caterpillars, I would line the jars up in Dad's tool shed. There they would sit in the coolness and change from caterpillars to cocoons.

In another two weeks, they would undergo another change and become beautiful butterflies.

On that sunny spring morning, as I stood under the clothesline, I could not find a single caterpillar. I asked my mother why.

Well, without a blink she turned and said to me, "Why don't you pray and ask God to bring the caterpillars?"

I will always remember that moment!
My mother had never said anything like
that before and it took me by surprise.

I went to my bedroom and got
down on my knees. I had never
talked to God before.

"Please, God, bring the caterpillars.
You know it's my favorite thing to watch
them become cocoons and then finally set
the beautiful butterflies free!
Thank you, God."

I went to bed that night excited,
wondering if God had heard me.

Upon waking up, I couldn't wait to see
if there were any furry caterpillars
waiting for me under the trees. As I
hurried to get my play clothes on,
I heard my mother calling.

She was shouting,
"Honey! Quick, come outside.
You won't believe this!!"

I dashed outside. Mom was standing at
the clothesline. Her eyes were wide and
she was smiling. I wondered why. She
turned her face toward the garage
and I followed her gaze.

It was then that I saw the miracle. . .

One whole side of the garage was completely covered with my wonderful caterpillars! Little, fuzzy bodies inched and suctioned their clingy feet all over the stucco wall.

My mother and I just stood there staring. It was so amazing, I wondered if this could be real.

I asked myself, why would the
caterpillars appear here of all places?
Usually they were crawling in the
trees or creeping across the ground.

I was standing in the exact same spot
when my mother had told me 'Go pray'.
This was no accident.
God had heard my prayer.

God loves to hear little children speak to Him
and He delights in answering their prayers.

Even the prayers of ordinary little girls
who are crazy about bugs and butterflies.

"Let the little children come to me, and
do not hinder them, for the kingdom of
heaven belongs to such as these."

MATTHEW 19:14

Questions for Family Discussion

Why should people pray?

Did you know that God hears all of your prayers? What evidence have you seen or felt that tells you this is so?

How come when we pray to God he doesn't always seem to answer?

Do you think miracles still happen today? In what way?

Think about your life. Are there things, people or events that show you how God loves you?

How can you have a strong, loving relationship with Jesus?

About the Author

Lurene Rascon was born in Needles, CA and now lives in Northern California with her husband. She is the mother of two beautiful daughters. Her interests include cooking, traveling and watching for God's little miracles along the road of life.

You may contact her at: lurenerascon.com

About the Illustrator

McKenna Zacher is a 14 year old freshman. She is an honor student with a passion for creativity. She loves to write, paint, draw and play Disney songs on the piano. Jesus Christ is her Lord and Savior.

38544848R00021

Made in the USA
Charleston, SC
09 February 2015